HYMNS OF THE FAITHFUL SERIES

PENTECOST TRINITY

WRITTEN BY

Richard Resch

CPH

Concordia Publishing House

Series editor: Thomas J. Doyle

This publication is available in braille and in large print for the visually impaired. Write to the Library for the Blind, 1333 S. Kirkwood Rd., St. Louis, MO 63122-7295; or call 1-800-433-3954.

Copyright © 1999 Concordia Publishing House
3558 S. Jefferson Avenue, St. Louis, MO 63118-3968
Manufactured in the United States of America

1   2   3   4   5   6   7   8   9   10   08   07   06   05   04   03   02   01   00   99

Contents

HYMN 1

Beautiful Savior

Page 4

HYMN 2

Praise God, from Whom All Blessings Flow

Page 7

HYMN 3

Praise to the Lord, the Almighty

Page 10

HYMN 4

Holy Spirit, Ever Dwelling

Page 13

HYMN 5

Baptized into Your Name Most Holy

Page 16

HYMN 6

Holy God, We Praise Your Name

Page 19

Beautiful Savior

Focus

"Beauty is in the eye of the beholder."

1. What might motivate someone to speak these words?

2. Why is *beautiful* an appropriate word to describe the person and work of Jesus?

3. How are the words of the hymn "Beautiful Savior" a confession of faith for the Christian "beholder"?

Inform

Sing "Beautiful Savior" (*LW* 507).

1. *Beautiful Savior, King of creation,*
   Son of God and Son of Man!
   Truly I'd love Thee, Truly I'd serve Thee,
   Light of my soul, my joy, my crown.

2. *Fair are the meadows, Fair are the woodlands,*
   Robed in flow'rs of blooming spring;
   Jesus is fairer, Jesus is purer,
   He makes our sorr'wing spirit sing.

3. *Fair is the sunshine, Fair is the moonlight,*
   Bright the sparkling stars on high;
   Jesus shines brighter, Jesus shines purer
   Than all the angels in the sky.

4. *Beautiful Savior, Lord of the nations,*
   Son of God and Son of Man!
   Glory and honor, Praise, adoration
   Now and forevermore be Thine!

1. Read Isaiah 4:2–6. These verses speak of a future "beauty"—a beauty that comes from the Branch of the Lord. What future beauty does the Lord promise? Underline those words or phrases that describe the blessings God will provide to His people.

2. Read again the stanzas of "Beautiful Savior." How are the words an appropriate response of faith by a people who have the beauty promised in Isaiah and fulfilled through their Savior, Jesus Christ? Circle those words of the hymn that describe the characteristics of the "beautiful Savior." Underline those words that describe the response of those who confess Jesus as Lord and Savior.

Connect

1. How has the beautiful Savior made you, once ugly due to sin, beautiful?

2. What might you say to someone who asked you the reason you describe Jesus as beautiful?

3. List other words you might use to describe Jesus. Write a prayer of thanksgiving and praise using these words.

Vision

As you wake this week, sing or speak the stanzas of "Beautiful Savior." Also, sing or speak the words of the hymn before you go to bed. Why are the words of this hymn an appropriate way to begin and end each day?

Beautiful Savior

Gesangbuch, Münster, 1677
Tr. Joseph A. Seiss, 1823–1904

SCHÖNSTER HERR JESU
Silesian folk tune, 1842

1 Beau - ti - ful Sav - ior, King of cre - a - tion,
2 Fair are the mead - ows, Fair are the wood - lands,
3 Fair is the sun - shine, Fair is the moon - light,
4 Beau - ti - ful Sav - ior, Lord of the na - tions,

Son of God and Son of Man!
Robed in flow'rs of bloom - ing spring;
Bright the spar - kling stars on high;
Son of God and Son of Man!

Tru - ly I'd love Thee, Tru - ly I'd serve Thee,
Je - sus is fair - er, Je - sus is pur - er,
Je - sus shines bright - er, Je - sus shines pur - er
Glo - ry and hon - or, Praise, ad - o - ra - tion

Light of my soul, my joy, my crown.
He makes our sor - r'wing spir - it sing.
Than all the an - gels in the sky.
Now and for - ev - er - more be Thine!

Praise God, from Whom All Blessings Flow

Focus

1. Describe a situation in which you experienced some type of an outburst.

2. What kind of outburst might you have when you think about God's love for you in Christ Jesus?

Inform

Sing together "Praise God, from Whom All Blessings Flow" (*LW* 461).

Praise God, from whom all blessings flow;
Praise Him, all creatures here below;
Praise Him above, O heav'nly host;
Praise Father, Son, and Holy Ghost.

1. Read one or more of the following psalms: Psalm 146; 147; 148; 149. Now read Psalm 150. Why might you describe these psalms as an outburst of praise?

2. What reasons are provided in these psalms for outbursts of praise?

3. Read again the words of "Praise God, from Whom All Blessings Flow." How is this hymn a summary of Psalms 146–150?

Connect

1. List specific blessings for which you have reason to praise God.

2. If you were to add a second stanza to the hymn, what thoughts or ideas would you include?

3. How might the final line of the hymn not only provide you the opportunity to praise God the Father for creating and sustaining your life, God the Son for redeeming you, and God the Holy Spirit for bringing you to faith and strengthening your faith, but also serve as a reminder of your Baptism?

Vision

We respond to God's love for us in Christ in our words and by our actions. Consider this week how your works of love are outbursts of praise.

Praise God, from Whom All Blessings Flow

Thomas Ken, 1637–1711

OLD HUNDREDTH
Louis Bourgeois, c. 1510–c. 1561

Praise God, from whom all bless-ings flow; Praise Him, all crea-tures here be-low;

Praise Him a-bove, O heav'n-ly host; Praise Fa-ther, Son, and Ho - ly Ghost.

Praise to the Lord, the Almighty

Focus

"And all the people said, 'Amen!' "

1. What is the significance of the word *amen?*

2. What events in your life cause you to pause and to say, "Amen!"?

Inform

Sing together "Praise to the Lord, the Almighty" (*LW* 444).

1. *Praise to the Lord, the Almighty, the King of creation!*
    O my soul, praise Him, for He is your health and salvation!
    Let all who hear Now to His temple draw near,
    Joining in glad adoration!

2. *Praise to the Lord, who o'er all things is wondrously reigning*
    And, as on wings of an eagle, uplifting, sustaining.
    Have you not seen All that is needful has been
    Sent by His gracious ordaining?

3. *Praise to the Lord, who will prosper your work and defend you;*
    Surely His goodness and mercy shall daily attend you.
    Ponder anew What the Almighty can do
    As with His love He befriends you.

4. *Praise to the Lord! Oh, let all that is in me adore Him!*
    All that has life and breath, come now with praises before Him!
    Let the amen Sound from His people again.
    Gladly forever adore Him!

1. Underline the words or phrases from the hymn that describe what God has done to give us reason to respond, "Amen."

2. Circle those words or phrases that describe how we respond to all that God has done for us.

3. Read any or all of the textual sources for the hymn: 1 Chronicles 16:23–36; Ezra 3:11; Nehemiah 9:6; Psalm 91:4; 103:1–11; 150; Isaiah 40:21. How adequately does the hymn reflect that which is revealed in the Scripture references? What reasons do these Scripture references provide as the motivation to respond, "Amen"?

Connect

1. How might you demonstrate an "amen" to God's love for you in Jesus by your words and in your actions. Be specific.

2. How might your "amen" of praise provide a witness of faith to others?

3. The greatest reason for "amen" occurred when Jesus died on the cross for your sins. Some have criticized this hymn for not clearly speaking of God's love in Jesus. What do you think? If time permits write an additional stanza to the hymn that focuses on the crucified and risen Jesus.

Vision

Meditate on the many blessings God provides for you. As you consider each blessing, speak aloud, "Amen." Take time this week to tell a friend or loved one the "amen" of God's love.

Praise to the Lord, the Almighty

Joachim Neander, 1650–80
Tr. Catherine Winkworth, 1829–78, alt.

LOBE DEN HERREN
Ernewertes Gesangbuch, Stralsund, 1665

1 Praise to the Lord, the Al - might - y, the King of cre - a - tion! O my soul, praise Him, for He is your health and sal - va - tion! Let all who hear Now to His tem - ple draw near, Join-ing in glad ad - o - ra - tion!

2 Praise to the Lord, who o'er all things is won - drous - ly reign - ing And, as on wings of an ea - gle, up - lift - ing, sus - tain - ing. Have you not seen All that is Sent by His gra-cious or - dain - ing?

3 Praise to the Lord, who will pros - per your work and de - fend you; Sure - ly His good - ness and mer - cy shall dai - ly at - tend you. Pon - der a - new What the Al- might - y can do As with His love He be - friends you.

4 Praise to the Lord! Oh, let all that is in me a - dore Him! All that has life and breath, come now with prais - es be - fore Him! Let the a - men Sound from His peo - ple a - gain. Glad - ly for - ev - er a - dore Him!

12

Holy Spirit, Ever Dwelling

Focus

1. A *dwelling* is a place of residence. What are some of the different types of dwellings in which people might take up residence?

2. What makes a dwelling a home, rather than simply a place of residence?

Inform

Sing together "Holy Spirit, Ever Dwelling" (*LW* 164).

1. *Holy Spirit, ever dwelling*
   In the holiest realms of light;
   Holy Spirit, ever brooding
   O'er a world of gloom and night;
   Holy Spirit, ever raising
   Those of earth to thrones on high;
   Living, life-imparting Spirit,
   You we praise and magnify.

2. *Holy Spirit, ever living*
   As the Church's very life;
   Holy Spirit, ever striving
   Through us in a ceaseless strife;
   Holy Spirit, ever forming
   In the Church the mind of Christ:
   You we praise with endless worship
   For Your gifts and fruits unpriced.

3. *Holy Spirit, ever working*
   Through the Church's ministry;
   Quick'ning, strength'ning, and absolving,
   Setting captive sinners free;
   Holy Spirit, ever binding
   Age to age and soul to soul
   In communion never ending,
   You we worship and extol.

Through Holy Baptism the Holy Spirit dwells in us. That is, the Holy Spirit has taken residence, made His home in us.

1. Read 1 Corinthians 2:9–16. How are we changed when the Holy Spirit dwells in us? What does the Holy Spirit enable us to do?

2. Now read Acts 2:1–4. How were those who were filled with the Holy Spirit affected? Skim Acts 2:14–41. How did the Holy Spirit change Peter? For help, see Mark 14:66–72.

3. Why is this an appropriate hymn to sing on Pentecost?

4. Underline the words or phrases in the hymn that indicate the effect of the Holy Spirit dwelling in people. How does the Holy Spirit change people? What does the Holy Spirit enable and empower people to do?

Connect

1. Describe the day of your Baptism. How did the Holy Spirit change you?

2. How might "Holy Spirit, Ever Dwelling" be an appropriate hymn to sing at a Baptism? as you remember your Baptism?

3. How might you describe the significance of the Holy Spirit dwelling in you? Why might this be an important witness of faith to others?

Vision

Remember your Baptism—its significance and blessings for you as you sing or speak the hymn each morning during the coming week as you awake. Now consider the peace you have because the Holy Spirit dwells in you.

Holy Spirit, Ever Dwelling

Timothy Rees, 1874–1939, alt.

IN BABILONE
Dutch folk tune, 18th cent.

1 Ho-ly Spir-it, ev-er dwell-ing In the ho-liest realms of light;
2 Ho-ly Spir-it, ev-er liv-ing As the Church's ver-y life;
3 Ho-ly Spir-it, ev-er work-ing Through the Church's min-is-try;

Ho - ly Spir - it, ev - er brood-ing O'er a world of gloom and night;
Ho - ly Spir - it, ev - er striv-ing Through us in a cease-less strife;
Quick-'ning, strength-'ning, and ab-solv-ing, Set-ting cap-tive sin-ners free;

Ho-ly Spir-it, ev-er rais-ing Those of earth to thrones on high;
Ho-ly Spir-it, ev-er form-ing In the Church the mind of Christ:
Ho-ly Spir-it, ev-er bind-ing Age to age and soul to soul

Liv-ing, life-im-part-ing Spir-it, You we praise and mag-ni-fy.
You we praise with end-less wor-ship For Your gifts and fruits un-priced.
In com-mu-nion nev-er end-ing, You we wor-ship and ex-tol.

Baptized into Your Name Most Holy

Focus

1. What benefits does a child receive when she or he is adopted?

2. What has an infant child done in order to earn these benefits?

3. Compare that which a child receives when adopted to that which is received in Holy Baptism.

Inform

Sing together "Baptized into Your Name Most Holy" (LW 224).

1. Baptized into Your name most holy,
   O Father, Son, and Holy Ghost,
   I claim a place, though weak and lowly,
   Among Your seed, Your chosen host.
   Buried with Christ and dead to sin,
   I have Your Spirit now within.

2. My loving Father, here You take me
   Henceforth to be Your child and heir;
   My faithful Savior, here You make me
   The fruit of all Your sorrows share;
   O Holy Ghost, You comfort me
   Though threat'ning clouds around I see.

3. O faithful God, You never fail me;
   Your cov'nant surely will abide.
   Let not eternal death assail me
   Should I transgress it on my side!
   Have mercy when I come defiled;
   Forgive, lift up, restore Your child.

4. All that I am and love most dearly,
   Receive it all, O Lord, from me.
   Oh, let me make my vows sincerely,
   And help me Your own child to be!
   Let nothing that I am or own
   Serve any will but Yours alone.

1. Read Matthew 28:19–20. How important is Holy Baptism? Why?

2. Now read Galatians 3:26–29. What does St. Paul list as benefits and blessings of Holy Baptism? In Holy Baptism all people take on one name—Christ(ian). What is the significance of adoption as God's children through faith in Jesus Christ?

3. "Baptized into Your Name Most Holy" is one of the favorite hymns sung before, during, or after a Baptism. How are the words of this hymn an appropriate description of God's work in Holy Baptism? of the blessings received in Holy Baptism? How might this hymn be a strong witness to unbelievers of God's love in Christ Jesus? What does it tell us about the power of God's love to make all people one?

Connect

1. What occurred for you and to you when you were baptized? Begin your response with "God ..."

2. Why is it important that "we remember daily" our Baptism?

3. Use the adoption analogy to describe to a friend or loved one what happened at your Baptism.

Vision

Meditate on the words of this hymn. Give thanks to God for the blessings and power He provided to you on the day of your Baptism. Praise God that through His adoption you receive daily power to live as His child.

Baptized into Your Name Most Holy

Johann J. Rambach, 1693–1735
Tr. Catherine Winkworth, 1829–78, alt.

O DASS ICH TAUSEND ZUNGEN HÄTTE
Kornelius Heinrich Dretzel, 1697–1775

1 Bap-tized in - to Your name most ho - ly, O Fa - ther, Son, and
2 My lov - ing Fa - ther, here You take me Hence-forth to be Your
3 O faith-ful God, You nev - er fail me; Your cov-'nant sure - ly
4 All that I am and love most dear - ly, Re - ceive it all, O

Ho - ly Ghost, I claim a place, though weak and low - ly,
child and heir; My faith-ful Sav - ior, here You make me
will a - bide. Let not e - ter - nal death as - sail me
Lord, from me. Oh, let me make my vows sin - cere - ly,

A - mong Your seed, Your cho - sen host. Bur - ied with Christ and
The fruit of all Your sor - rows share; O Ho - ly Ghost, You
Should I trans - gress it on my side! Have mer - cy when I
And help me Your own child to be! Let noth-ing that I

dead to sin, I have Your Spir - it now with - in.
com - fort me Though threat-'ning clouds a - round I see.
come de - filed; For - give, lift up, re - store Your child.
am or own Serve an - y will but Yours a - lone.

Study Sheet 6
Holy God, We Praise Your Name

Focus

1. All people need praise and affirmation. For what might you praise someone? For what has someone recently praised you?

2. How does it make you feel when you receive praise from someone? give praise to someone?

Inform

Sing together "Holy God, We Praise Your Name" (LW 171).

1. Holy God, we praise Your name;
   Lord of all, we bow before You.
   All on earth Your scepter claim,
   All in heav'n above adore You.
   Infinite Your vast domain,
   Everlasting is Your reign.

2. Hark! The glad celestial hymn
   Angel choirs above are raising;
   Cherubim and seraphim,
   In unceasing chorus praising,
   Fill the heav'ns with sweet accord:
   "Holy, holy, holy Lord!"

3. Lo, the apostolic train
   Join Your sacred name to hallow;
   Prophets swell the glad refrain,
   And the white-robed martyrs follow;
   And from morn to set of sun
   Through the Church the song goes on.

4. You are King of Glory, Christ;
   Son of God, yet born of Mary.
   For us sinners sacrificed,
   As to death a Tributary,
   First to break the bars of death,
   You have opened heav'n to faith.

5. Holy Father, holy Son,
   Holy Spirit, three we name You,
   Though in essence only one;
   Undivided God we claim You
   And, adoring, bend the knee
   While we own the mystery.

1. Read the textual sources for this hymn: Psalm 30:1–4; 105:1–4; 111:2–9; Isaiah 6:2–3; Luke 2:13–14; Revelation 7:9–12. What do each of these Scripture references have in common? What reasons are included in these verses for praising God?

2. List those things for which you have reason to praise God. Now, underline those words or phrases from the hymn that enumerate reasons to praise God. How does your list compare to the list of the hymn writer?

3. The words of this hymn have been present or used in one form or another by the church as the Te Deum (You, God, we praise) for more than 1,500 years. What enduring qualities do the words of this hymn have?

Connect

1. This well-loved hymn has been sung in worship services, at the funeral of President John F. Kennedy, and following the historic Mass celebrated by Pope Paul VI on October 4, 1965, in Yankee Stadium in New York City. Review the words of the hymn. What makes the words appropriate for so many different occasions? Can you think of other occasions when the use of this hymn would be appropriate?

2. How does the singing of this hymn provide you an opportunity to confess your faith in Christ Jesus?

3. Write a personalized stanza for the hymn. Begin the stanza, "Holy God, I praise Your name ..."

Vision

This week, spend time reviewing each of the three major confessions of faith used throughout the ages of the Christian Church—the Apostles' Creed; Nicene Creed; Athanasian Creed. Martin Luther considered the Te Deum second only to these creeds as a confession of faith. Compare the words of the hymn to the creeds. Confess daily the words of the hymn.

Holy God, We Praise Your Name

Source unknown
Tr. Clarence A. Walworth, 1820–1900, alt.

GROSSER GOTT
Maria Theresa, *Katholisches Gesangbuch*, 1774

1 Ho - ly God, we praise Your name; Lord of all, we
2 Hark! The glad ce - les - tial hymn An - gel choirs a -
3 Lo, the ap - os - tol - ic train Join Your sa - cred
4 You are King of Glo - ry, Christ; Son of God, yet

bow be - fore You. All on earth Your scep - ter claim,
bove are rais - ing; Cher - u - bim and ser - a - phim,
name to hal - low; Proph - ets swell the glad re - frain,
born of Mar - y. For us sin - ners sac - ri - ficed,

All in heav'n a - bove a - dore You. In - fi - nite Your
In un - ceas - ing cho - rus prais - ing, Fill the heav'ns with
And the white - robed mar - tyrs fol - low; And from morn to
As to death a Trib - u - tar - y, First to break the

vast do - main, Ev - er - last - ing is Your reign.
sweet ac - cord: "Ho - ly, ho - ly, ho - ly Lord!"
set of sun Through the Church the song goes on.
bars of death, You have o - pened heav'n to faith.

5 Holy Father, holy Son,
Holy Spirit, three we name You,
Though in essence only one;
Undivided God we claim You
And, adoring, bend the knee
While we own the mystery.